THE SEPARATISTS

WRITTEN BY HANNAH DOLAN, ELIZABETH DOWSETT,
CLARE HIBBERT, SHARI LAST, AND VICTORIA TAYLOR

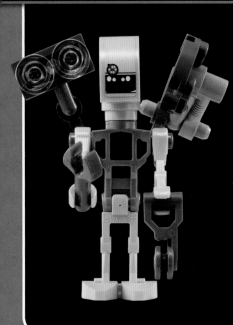

INTRODUCTION

The rebellious Separatists cause trouble accross the LEGO® *Star Wars* galaxy. Find out about this dangerous group—from the deadly Destroyer Droid to the bumbling Battle Droid.

HOW TO USE THIS BOOK

These amazing minifigures are ordered according to the *Star Wars*™ property in which they first appeared or mostly featured. Tabs at the top of each page indicate which properties this minifgure appears in. As most *Star Wars* characters appear in the wider universe of Legends, that tab is highlighted only if a minifigure appears in an Legends set. The Clone Wars tab has not been highlighted if the character has a separate Clone Wars minifigure.

This book also includes variants of featured minifigures, which are the same character, but have some modifications that make them different in some way.

Contents

The battle droid minifigure has been released in vast numbers in the LEGO *Star Wars* galaxy, appearing in around 60 LEGO® sets to date. The Separatist soldier relies on quantity, not skill, to defeat its enemy. It cannot think independently and its firing accuracy is poor—partly because the minifigure could not hold a blaster correctly until 2007!

Battle Droid
SEPARATIST FOOT SOLDIER

LEGO head and chest pieces were specially created for the battle droid minifigure

As with normal LEGO minifigures, the battle droid is only articulated at the shoulder, but its two arms are not identical

Regular infantry battle droids have plain tan torsos, but command officers have colored torsos to denote rank

SE-14 blaster pistol

Armed arm
Two variants of the battle droid minifigure cannot hold a blaster vertically. However, since 2007, the battle droid has had one straight, or turned, arm so the minifigure can hold a gun correctly.

The battle droid's feet and legs are one LEGO piece

STAR VARIANTS

Traveling light
First appearing in the 1999 Naboo Fighter (set 7141), this battle droid now comes in a total of 16 LEGO sets. He is near-identical to the battle droid with the backpack, but he is stationed on the ground, so he doesn't need somewhere to store a parachute!

Backpack
Two 1999–2000 LEGO sets have included this battle droid with a backpack: Naboo Swamp (set 7121) and LEGO *Star Wars* #4 Battle Droid Minifigure Pack (set 3343). It also appears in the Tank Droid (set 75015).

One of a kind
This droid is unique to the 2008 Droid Gunship (set 7678), which contains a pair. It is the only straight-armed battle droid without a backpack whose hands both face the front.

DATA FILE
YEAR: 2007
FIRST SET: 7662 MTT
NO. OF SETS: 8
PIECES: 5
ACCESSORIES: Blaster

STAR VARIANTS

Simple start

The original droideka figure from 2002 has a much simpler design than the 2007 variant, but its 26 pieces still capture the droid's distinctive shape.

Droid redesign

The 2007 version of the destroyer droid is unique to one set: Trade Federation MTT (set 7662). This was the first to use Viking helmet horns as foot pieces.

Sniper droid

This droideka appears in AT-RT (set 75002) from 2013. Unlike the regular destroyer droids, it features rear armor panels.

In 2002, the first destroyer droid rolled into the world of LEGO *Star Wars*. Also known as a droideka, this robotic ball of firepower is a key part of the Separatists' ground forces. With its curved spine and tripod feet, the droid posed a challenge to LEGO designers. The most recent version comes under fire from a Republic AV-7 Anti-Vehicle cannon (set 75045).

Moveable antenna piece first appeared in 1985 as a train track lever switch

Arm piece mold is also used for battle droids' arms

Blaster energizer

Foot piece appears in other LEGO sets as horns on Viking helmets. An earlier, almost identical variant, features dark silver arms

Destroyer Droid
ROLLING FIREPOWER

LEGO® Technic

As well as two minifigures, the destroyer droid has also been made as a 567-piece LEGO Technic model in 2000 (set 8002). When spun across the floor, the LEGO droid rolls and then unfurls into its attack position.

A variant from Naboo Starfighter (set 7877) of this minifigure has black barbs

DATA FILE

YEAR: 2014
FIRST SET: 75045 Republic AV-7 Anti-Vehicle Cannon
NO. OF SETS: 2
PIECES: 28
ACCESSORIES: None

Although all battle droids are structurally identical and made from the same LEGO pieces, specialist battle droids are fitted with a colored torso to identify their function. These droids are chosen for certain roles to increase the army's efficiency. They are found in a select few LEGO sets where their specific skills are required.

This variant of the battle droid commander has an all-yellow torso piece

Into battle
Yellow coloring on the chest signifies that this droid is a battle droid commander. One commander, OOM-9, was responsible for leading the entire battle droid army at the Battle of the Great Grass Plains.

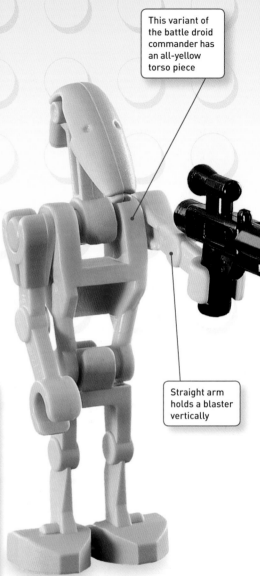

Straight arm holds a blaster vertically

Battle Droids
SPECIALISTS

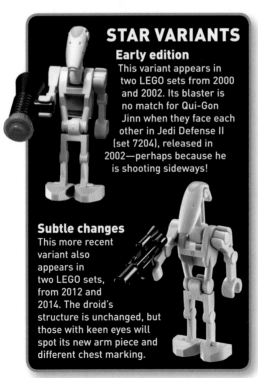

STAR VARIANTS

Early edition
This variant appears in two LEGO sets from 2000 and 2002. Its blaster is no match for Qui-Gon Jinn when they face each other in Jedi Defense II (set 7204), released in 2002—perhaps because he is shooting sideways!

Subtle changes
This more recent variant also appears in two LEGO sets, from 2012 and 2014. The droid's structure is unchanged, but those with keen eyes will spot its new arm piece and different chest marking.

DATA FILE

NAME: Battle droid commander
YEAR: 2008
FIRST SET: 7670 Hailfire Droid & Spider Droid
NO. OF SETS: 2
PIECES: 5
ACCESSORIES: Blaster

Battle colors

Specialist battle droids have had varying amounts of color on their torsos since their first release in 2000. The earliest variants have mostly tan torsos with only small patches of color, while others have full-color torsos.

The security battle droid has a red tip on the back of its head piece. This detail is first seen on the 2011 design

Security battle droids provide extra protection onboard starships

Torso piece has dark red markings

DATA FILE

NAME: Security battle droid
YEAR: 2014
FIRST SET: 75044 Droid Tri-Fighter
NO. OF SETS: 1
PIECES: 5
ACCESSORIES: Blaster

Molded head piece is only found in LEGO *Star Wars* sets

Made to match

All these battle droids are designed to look like their Geonosian creators—with elongated limbs and faces. LEGO *Star Wars* battle droids resemble their movie counterparts by putting extra emphasis on these features.

The battle droid pilot is identified by blue markings

DATA FILE

NAME: Battle droid pilot
YEAR: 2014
FIRST SET: 75058 MTT
NO. OF SETS: 4
PIECES: 5
ACCESSORIES: Blaster

Battle Droids
SPECIALISTS

Enigmatic minifigure Count Dooku was once a Jedi Master, but he has fallen to the dark side. He now lurks in the shadows of the LEGO *Star Wars* galaxy. The minifigure was updated in 2013 and given an expressive reversible head. On this side is the count's look of grim concentration; on the reverse, he sports an evil, toothy grin.

STAR VARIANT

First count

For more than a decade, the only Episode II Count Dooku minifigure was the 2002 version from Jedi Duel (set 7103). There is also a Clone Wars version.

Curved lightsaber

As befits a man of his wealth and status, Count Dooku wields a custom-made lightsaber with a curved metallic hilt. Exclusive to Dooku, the weapon also appears with his 2009 Clone Wars minifigure in Count Dooku's Solar Sailer (set 7752).

Dooku is the only LEGO *Star Wars* minifigure with this head, but it appears on two Saruman minifigures from the LEGO® *Lord of the Rings*™ theme

Count Dooku
EVIL COUNT OF SERENNO

DATA FILE

YEAR: 2013
FIRST SET: 75017 Duel on Geonosis
NO. OF SETS: 1
PIECES: 5
ACCESSORIES: Cape, lightsaber, force lightning

Only Count Dooku's minifigure has this torso printing, with its cape clasp and brown belt

This is a standard LEGO minifigure cape. It acts as a symbol of Dooku's prestige as Count of Serenno

Flesh facts

The recent Dooku has realistic flesh colored skin, but the 2002 version is yellow. That is because the LEGO Group did not produce minifigures with lighter flesh until 2004—all the early Episode II minifigures are yellow.

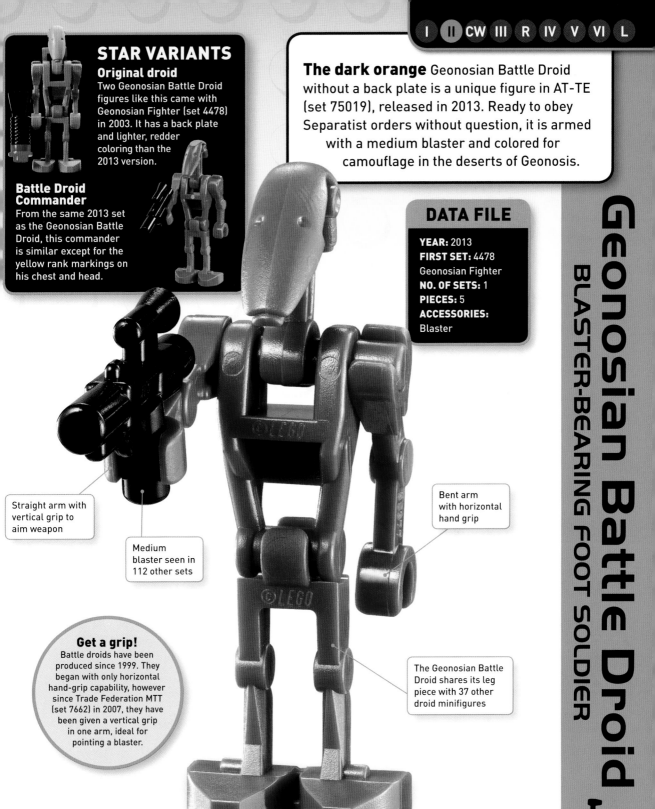

STAR VARIANTS

Original droid
Two Geonosian Battle Droid figures like this came with Geonosian Fighter (set 4478) in 2003. It has a back plate and lighter, redder coloring than the 2013 version.

Battle Droid Commander
From the same 2013 set as the Geonosian Battle Droid, this commander is similar except for the yellow rank markings on his chest and head.

The dark orange Geonosian Battle Droid without a back plate is a unique figure in AT-TE (set 75019), released in 2013. Ready to obey Separatist orders without question, it is armed with a medium blaster and colored for camouflage in the deserts of Geonosis.

DATA FILE

YEAR: 2013
FIRST SET: 4478 Geonosian Fighter
NO. OF SETS: 1
PIECES: 5
ACCESSORIES: Blaster

Geonosian Battle Droid
BLASTER-BEARING FOOT SOLDIER

Straight arm with vertical grip to aim weapon

Medium blaster seen in 112 other sets

Bent arm with horizontal hand grip

Get a grip!
Battle droids have been produced since 1999. They began with only horizontal hand-grip capability, however since Trade Federation MTT (set 7662) in 2007, they have been given a vertical grip in one arm, ideal for pointing a blaster.

The Geonosian Battle Droid shares its leg piece with 37 other droid minifigures

9

Super Battle Droid
WALKING WEAPONRY

Bigger, bulkier, and more blaster-proof than standard battle droids, super battle droids are a force to be reckoned with. Not only are they physically stronger than their spindlier cousins, but they also have more brainpower. Three variants of the hulking super battle droid minifigure have been made—each more intimidating than the last.

Specially molded head-and-body piece is used for all three variants of the super battle droid

Technical droid
Like the destroyer droid, the super battle droid has gone beyond its minifigure beginnings and been created as a LEGO® Technic set. The robotic figure, released in 2002, is made from 379 technical parts.

Arms clip to shoulder pieces with same grip as minifigures' hands

STAR VARIANTS

Blue beginnings

The first super battle droid minifigure is metal-blue and was released in 2002. Two come with the Republic Gunship (set 7163).

Blast off
In 2009, the super battle droid swapped one of its arms for a unique piece with a blaster molded into it. This third variant of the droid appears in two LEGO sets.

Hands can grasp LEGO blaster weapons

Pearlized, dark gray body

Leg piece is unique to LEGO *Star Wars*. It is also found on the MagnaGuard (p.14) the TX-20 tactical droid (p.17), and the commando droid (p.19)

Thin legs create a small target for enemy fire

DATA FILE
YEAR: 2014
FIRST SET: 7654 Droids Battle Pack
NO. OF SETS: 11
PIECES: 4
ACCESSORIES: None

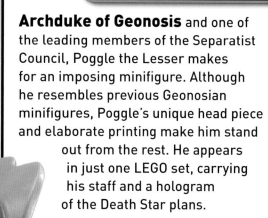

Duel on Geonosis (set 75017)
Poggle can only be found in this 2013 LEGO set. While Count Dooku battles Yoda in his secret Geonosis hangar, cowardly Poggle lurks in the background.

Archduke of Geonosis and one of the leading members of the Separatist Council, Poggle the Lesser makes for an imposing minifigure. Although he resembles previous Geonosian minifigures, Poggle's unique head piece and elaborate printing make him stand out from the rest. He appears in just one LEGO set, carrying his staff and a hologram of the Death Star plans.

Crown-like head crest

Unique head piece molding shows Poggle's long beard and tendrils, signs of his age and status

Same wing pieces as the winged Geonosian Warrior (p.21)

DATA FILE

YEAR: 2013
FIRST SET: 75017
Duel on Geonosis
NO. OF SETS: 1
PIECES: 4
ACCESSORIES:
Death Star hologram

Geonosian exoskeleton printing is continued on lower back of torso

Intricate gold and black details are symbols of royalty

Secret plans
Poggle's minifigure holds an orange hologram of the Geonosian-designed Death Star.

Poggle the Lesser
ARCHDUKE OF GEONOSIS

FA-4 Pilot Droid
DOOKU'S PERSONAL PILOT

The FA-4 pilot droid has been released as two very different minifigures. The 2009 version was all white and built mainly from battle droid parts. The 2013 version more accurately portrays the copper and silver wheeled droid. He chauffeurs Count Dooku in one set—and also pops up on his own in the 2013 LEGO *Star Wars* Advent Calendar.

Wide-set visual sensors provide a panoramic view during flight

Battle droid arm and torso are the only parts this version shares with 2009 version

Heads apart
While the original FA-4 minifigure used a LEGO skeleton foot as its head piece, the 2013 version has a commando droid's head piece with unique printing.

DATA FILE

YEAR: 2013
FIRST SET: 75017 Duel on Geonosis
NO. OF SETS: 2
PIECES: 9
ACCESSORIES: None

Wheeled base is a 1x3 plate with brown slopes on it

Duel on Geonosis (set 75017)
Count Dooku's personal FA-4 droid waits in Dooku's secret Geonosis hangar, ready to help his owner escape aboard his solar sailer.

General Grievous' Starfighter (set 8095)

The Clone Wars General Grievous minifigure first appeared in this set. His luxurious starfighter includes a medical room, lightsaber rack, an opening cockpit with controls, and hidden missiles.

General Grievous's cyborg minifigure was updated for LEGO Clone Wars in 2010. His four-armed minifigure now appears in two sets and is built entirely from exclusive pieces. But despite his top-to-toe minifigure makeover, Grievous is still his old self—a vicious villain with an untempered hatred of the Jedi.

Grievous's head piece resembles a mask he wore as a Kaleesh warlord. The classic Grievous minifigure has no face printing (p.26)

Grievous's four arms have hinged joints so they can be positioned in many ways

Grievous collects the lightsabers of his Jedi victims

Not a droid

Grievous hates being called a droid. He is a cyborg: part flesh, part metal. Grievous's classic minifigure (p.26) is built from some droid parts, but his Clone Wars minifigure is completely unique. Grievous would probably approve!

General Grievous
CLONE WARS CYBORG

DATA FILE

YEAR: 2010
FIRST SET: 8095 General Grievous' Starfighter
NO. OF SETS: 2
PIECES: 8
ACCESSORIES: Four lightsabers, blaster

Dark bluish-gray and tan colors are new to this Grievous minifigure

The MagnaGuard minifigure

is an advanced battle droid designed by General Grievous to pose a threat to any clone troopers or Jedi Knights that cross his path. Dressed to intimidate in a unique Kaleesh warrior cape and headwrap, the MagnaGuard carries an electrostaff that is resistant to lightsaber blades.

MagnaGuard Starfighter (set 7673)

Two MagnaGuards appear in this 2008 set. Their specialized starfighter has deadly flick-fire missiles. The MagnaGuards store their electrostaffs at the back of the ship's wings during flight.

Headwrap is integrated in the MagnaGuard's unique head piece

Glowing red photoreceptors

Torso piece was first seen on the MagnaGuard. Fellow Separatist droid A4-D (p.20) adopted it in 2010

Mechanical arm is in two parts

Only the MagnaGuard minifigure carries a powerful LEGO electrostaff

MagnaGuard
MECHANICAL MONSTER

DATA FILE

YEAR: 2008
FIRST SET: 7673 MagnaGuard Starfighter
NO. OF SETS: 2
PIECES: 9
ACCESSORIES: Electrostaff, cape

This large red round plate piece is a third photoreceptor

Cruel cape
The MagnaDroid is the only LEGO minifigure to feature this tan cloth cape with a tattered edge.

The super battle droid (p.10) and TX-20 (p.17) have the same mechanical legs

STAR VARIANT
Green Viceroy
The 2014 version of Nute has an updated head piece with olive-green skin and a sloping base piece with unique printing for his robes. His miter is the same mold used for the gray headdress below.

As the viceroy of the Trade Federation, Nute Gunray has a lot of power. But instead of working for the good of the LEGO *Star Wars* galaxy, this Neimoidian minifigure is motivated by greed. Nute's well-dressed but miserable minifigure is the only named member of his species to have been created in LEGO form. He appears in just four sets.

Iron deposits build up in Neimoidians, turning their eyes orange

Nute's elaborate official robes are printed on his unique torso

Nute's head piece is printed with his mottled, gray Neimoidian skin—and his perpetual frown

Gray, scaly Neimoidian hands

Metal badge in the shape of the official Trade Federation insignia

Nute's Viceroy robes are bright in color so he gets more attention than lesser officials

Nute Gunray
TRADE FEDERATION VICEROY

DATA FILE

YEAR: 2009
FIRST SET: 8036 Separatist Shuttle
NO. OF SETS: 2
PIECES: 4
ACCESSORIES: None

Count Dooku's personal pilot droid is the only one of his kind in LEGO *Star Wars*, but he is made up entirely of LEGO pieces seen on other minifigures. His body is made from battle droid parts, and his head is seen on skeletons in other LEGO themes, including Fantasy Era. The FA-4 model droid exclusively pilots Count Dooku's Solar Sailer (set 7752).

Count Dooku's Solar Sailer (set 7752)
The pilot droid sits on a sliding seat inside the working cockpit of Count Dooku's *Punworcca 116*-class interstellar sloop. He navigates through a rounded cockpit window.

Pilot Droid
COUNT DOOKU'S CHAUFFEUR

Head is actually made from a LEGO skeleton leg piece!

Leg head
The pilot droid's head can be found on many other minifigures, but it has never before been used as a head piece—it mostly functions as a leg piece on LEGO skeletons.

This white mechanical torso piece is commonly used on battle droids (pp.6–7)

The 2007 release of General Grievous's minifigure (p.26) has these same white mechanical arms, but his minifigure has four of them!

Some FA-4 pilot droids move around on wheels, but the LEGO FA-4 has white mechanical legs

DATA FILE

YEAR: 2009
FIRST SET: 7752 Count Dooku's Solar Sailer
NO. OF SETS: 1
PIECES: 5
ACCESSORIES: None

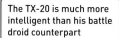

The TX-20 is much more intelligent than his battle droid counterpart

Tactical Droid TX-20 is a strategic planner and supervisor of Separatist troops stationed in Ryloth City. His unique minifigure made his debut in the 2011 LEGO Clone Wars set Mace Windu's Jedi Starfighter (set 7876). He has an unusual combined head-and-torso piece that is exclusive to his minifigure.

Unique Separatist symbol

Processing unit buried inside heavily armored torso to protect it when under fire from enemy forces

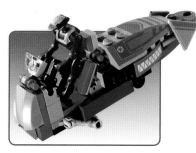

Mace Windu's Jedi Starfighter (set 7868)
The tactical droid zips around on his Separatist Flitknot speeder. He has a seat that allows him to comfortably perch and then jump out when he needs to.

Dark blue mechanical arm exclusive to TX-20

Legs are also seen on the super battle droid (p.10) and MagnaGuard (p.14) minifigures

TX-20
TACTICAL DROID

DATA FILE

YEAR: 2011
FIRST SET: 7868 Mace Windu's Jedi Starfighter
NO. OF SETS: 1
PIECES: 5
ACCESSORIES: None

Rocket Droid Commander
AIRBORNE DROID

The rocket droid commander is a specialist Separatist droid who leads a battalion of rocket battle droids. His minifigure has a rocketpack on his back and wears lightweight armor for space combat. This droid only appears in one LEGO set, where he uses his superior programming to attack the Republic.

DATA FILE

YEAR: 2010
FIRST SET: 80867
Droid Tri-Fighter
NO. OF SETS: 1
PIECES: 7
ACCESSORIES: Blaster

Receiver for central droid command signal

Unique head piece is the same mold as the battle droid minifigure (p.4), but with different coloring

One of the arm pieces has a hand that is turned 90 degrees so it can hold a blaster

Unusual jetpack
The rocket droid commander's jetpack is actually a LEGO binoculars piece. It is also used for the destroyer droid's blasters (p.5).

He uses the same E-5 blaster as regular battle droids

Yellow markings indicate rank of commander

Rocketpack clips onto his back

Same leg piece as the battle droid minifigure

Droid Tri-Fighter (set 8086)
The rocket droid commander is exclusive to this LEGO set. The set also comes with two rocket battle droid minifigures, which are the same as the commander, but without the yellow armor markings.

STAR VARIANT
Commando droid
The original commando droid has white eyes like its counterpart, but its face has dark tan printing, rather than black and white. It appeared for the first time in the Elite Clone Trooper and Commando Droid Battle Pack (set 9488), released in 2012.

The second of two commando droid minifigures, this 2013 version is notable for its striking face print, denoting its superior rank. More intelligent and dangerous than a standard battle droid, the commando droid captain leads its unit on missions of stealth. This deadly droid provides an adversary in the AT-RT (set 75002) which also contains Yoda and a 501st legion clone trooper.

Commando Droid Captain
LETHAL LEADER

Arm with vertical grip appears in 23 droid figures

LEGO Space skeleton arm piece with standard grip

Torso has reinforced droid armor plating

Dark brown coloring makes commando hard to spot at night

Leg power
These mechanical legs appear as part of seven different LEGO Star Wars droids, including the MagnaGuard (2008–9) and super battle droid (2007–14).

DATA FILE
YEAR: 2013
FIRST SET: 75002 AT-RT
NO. OF SETS: 1
PIECES: 5
ACCESSORIES: Blaster

A4-D is a sadistic medical droid and General Grievous's personal doctor in just one LEGO set. His minifigure is built out of standard droid parts, but with many medical modifications! Extra arms on A4-D's torso hold all manner of equipment, which he is more than happy to use—no matter how much trouble he causes!

DATA FILE

YEAR: 2010
FIRST SET: 8095 General Grievous' Starfighter
NO. OF SETS: 1
PIECES: 18
ACCESSORIES: Tools

A4-D
SADISTIC ROBOT DOCTOR

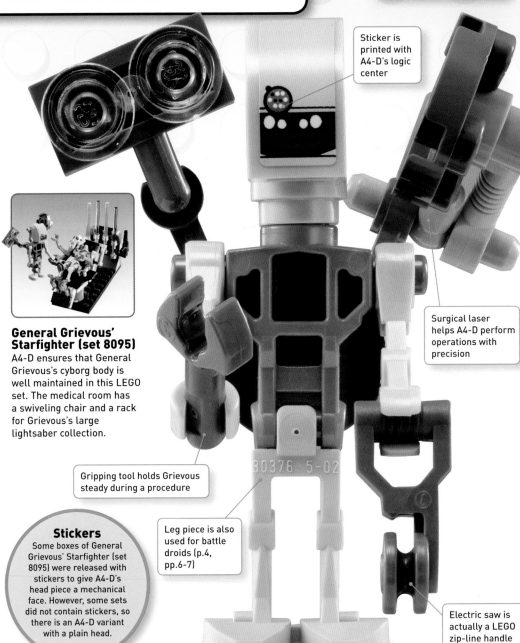

Sticker is printed with A4-D's logic center

Surgical laser helps A4-D perform operations with precision

Gripping tool holds Grievous steady during a procedure

Leg piece is also used for battle droids (p.4, pp.6-7)

Electric saw is actually a LEGO zip-line handle

General Grievous' Starfighter (set 8095)
A4-D ensures that General Grievous's cyborg body is well maintained in this LEGO set. The medical room has a swiveling chair and a rack for Grievous's large lightsaber collection.

Stickers
Some boxes of General Grievous' Starfighter (set 8095) were released with stickers to give A4-D's head piece a mechanical face. However, some sets did not contain stickers, so there is an A4-D variant with a plain head.

STAR VARIANT
Geonosian
The 2011 variant flies the Geonosian Starfighter (set 7959). He shares the same head, torso, and leg pieces as the later variant, but he does not have wings.

DATA FILE
YEAR: 2012
FIRST SET: 9491
Geonosian Cannon
NO. OF SETS: 1
PIECES: 4
ACCESSORIES: Blaster

The rocky outcrops of Geonosis house the hive colonies of an insectoid, hive-minded race, which is loyal to the Separatist cause. This 2012 Geonosian winged warrior operates a powerful cannon at the Battle of Geonosis. His head shape, shared with the 2011 variant, develops the original LEGO Geonosian head-mold.

Insectoid eyes bulge out of head piece

Chitin armor, with its composition of insect shell and animal skin, protects against the sonic energy weapons favored by Geonosians

Geonosian exoskeleton markings

Gold markings are typical of Geonosian decoration

Red iketa stones are symbols of war in Geonosian culture

Geonosian Warrior
WINGED DEFENDER

21

Back from the dead, this zombie is a unique figure, though there have been other versions of planet Geonosis's native insectoid race before—the first was the 2003 figure in the Geonosian Fighter (set 4478). Part of the Geonosian queen's personal guard, this zombie warrior can feel no pain and is controlled via a worm in his skull.

Modified Geonosian head piece with gray eyes to indicate undead status

Geonosian Cannon (set 9491)
A fearsome figure, the Geonosian zombie operates this cannon alongside a living Geonosian warrior. They fire powerful flick missiles to repel the clone army's attack.

Geonosian Zombie
CREEPY UNDEAD WARRIOR

Wicked wings
Transparent plastic wings with black and gray printing create a creepy shredded effect. No other figure has this spooky feature.

Armored insectoid exoskeleton made of chitin can be shed

Torso is a unique piece, based on the 2011 Geonosian pilot torso, but colored in the Geonosian zombie pattern

Sonic blaster

DATA FILE
YEAR: 2012
FIRST SET: 9491 Geonosian Cannon
NO. OF SETS: 1
PIECES: 4
ACCESSORIES: Blaster

Umbaran MHC (set 75013)

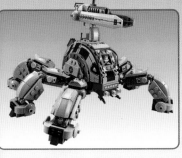

Seen in the Clone Wars, this massive mobile weapon has posable legs, a swiveling cannon, and a missile launcher. Its front and rear cockpits open to fit the soldier. The set has four minifigures, including Ahsoka Tano.

The Umbaran soldier fights on the Separatist side in the Clone Wars. His minifigure appears in only one 2013 set, the Umbaran MHC (Mobile Heavy Cannon) (set 75013). Born on a planet that is always in darkness, the soldier has pale skin, colored lavender by a special gas pumped into his helmet to increase his reaction speed and warlike attitude.

Space helmet appears on 27 LEGO minifigures, but only this once in LEGO *Star Wars* minifigures

Unique head piece printed with large purple eyes, white eyebrows, and a stern expression

Standard blaster

Dark sight
The Umbarans have special night vision and a great deal of detail has been used to draw attention to this minifigure's haunting eyes. They are purple with penetrating dark pupils—and a bold white gleam.

New torso piece features Umbaran armor printing which continues on the back

Protective gloves

Umbaran Soldier
NIGHT-SIGHTED MILITANT

DATA FILE
YEAR: 2013
FIRST SET: 75013 Umbaran MHC (Mobile Heavy Cannon)
NO OF SETS: 1
PIECES: 5
ACCESSORIES: Blaster

A powerful Jedi who falls to the dark side, General Pong Krell is the first Besalisk to appear as a LEGO minifigure. Krell is relentless and ferocious in battle. Being a Besalisk gives the general two main advantages: his height and his four arms, which allow him to wield the two double-bladed lightsabers that come with his set—the Z-95 Headhunter (set 75004) from 2013.

Double-bladed lightsabers in green and blue

New head and torso mold is a single piece

Z-95 Headhunter (set 75004)
Perfect for battling the Separatists in the dark skies above Umbara, this starfighter has a secret weapon—a spring-loaded LEGO Technic shooter.

Dark orange torso with Jedi robe

Jedi robe and white leg armor plates painted onto legs

Pong Krell
FOUR-ARMED FIGHTER

DATA FILE

YEAR: 2013
FIRST SET: 75004 Z-95 Headhunter
NO OF SETS: 1
PIECES: 3
ACCESSORIES: Twin double-bladed lightsabers

STAR VARIANT
Triple whammy
The original buzz droid stands on two mechanical legs. It appears in three LEGO *Star Wars* sets: Droid Tri-Fighter (set 7252) and Ultimate Space Battle (set 7283) from 2005, and Ahsoka's Starfighter and Droids from 2009 (set 7751).

Look out for this deadly LEGO buzz droid! Unleashed by the Separatists, this droid attaches itself to enemy starships with its legs and then destroys them with a powerful circular saw. Two equally deadly variants of the minifigure have wreaked havoc in five LEGO sets.

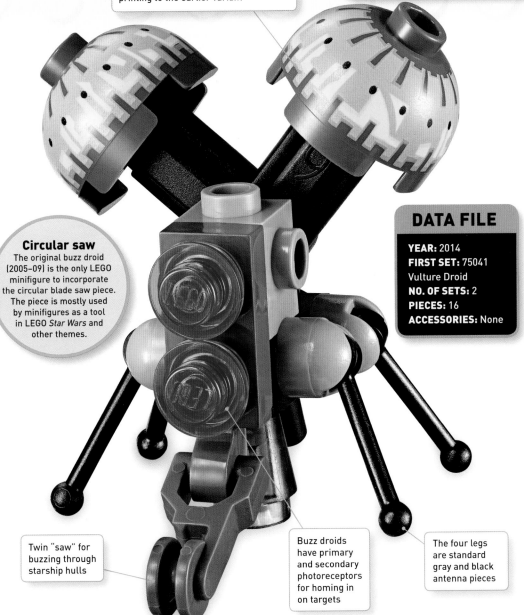

Shock-absorbing outer hull is unique to the 2014 buzz droid and has different printing to the earlier variant

Circular saw
The original buzz droid (2005–09) is the only LEGO minifigure to incorporate the circular blade saw piece. The piece is mostly used by minifigures as a tool in LEGO *Star Wars* and other themes.

DATA FILE
YEAR: 2014
FIRST SET: 75041 Vulture Droid
NO. OF SETS: 2
PIECES: 16
ACCESSORIES: None

Buzz Droid
DEADLY DROID

Twin "saw" for buzzing through starship hulls

Buzz droids have primary and secondary photoreceptors for homing in on targets

The four legs are standard gray and black antenna pieces

This vicious cyborg might look like a LEGO droid, but don't tell him that! He will react savagely, as his many victims will attest. General Grievous is Supreme Commander of the Droid Armies. His minifigure has four lightsabers—two blue and two green—to fill his four arms, making him more than a match for any Jedi!

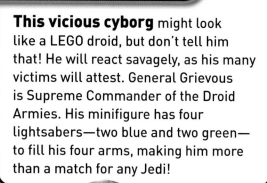

STAR VARIANT
Plain evil
There are two all-white Grievous minifigures. One wears a cape in the 2005 set General Grievous Chase (set 7255). The 2007 variant has no cape as he flies his starfighter (set 7656).

Grievous's rotting red and yellow eyes are printed on his head piece. The earlier variant has no face printing

General Grievous
CLONE WARS CYBORG

Grievous's four arms have hinged joints so they can be positioned in many ways

Grievous collects the lightsabers of his Jedi victims

Legs, torso, and head are the same as the Clone Wars variant (p.13), but with new colors and printing

DATA FILE
YEAR: 2014
FIRST SET: 75040 General Grievous' Wheel Bike
NO. OF SETS: 1
PIECES: 8
ACCESSORIES: 4 Lightsabers, electrostaff